COPING™

COPING WITH
SEXISM AND
MISOGYNY

Gloria G. Adams

Rosen
YA

Published in 2018 by The Rosen Publishing Group, Inc.
29 East 21st Street, New York, NY 10010

Library of Congress Cataloging-in-Publication Data

Names: Adams, Gloria G., author.
Title: Coping with sexism and misogyny / Gloria G. Adams.
Description: New York : Rosen Publishing, 2018 | Series: Coping | Audience: Grades 7–12. | Includes bibliographical references and index.
Identifiers: LCCN 2017018517 | ISBN 9781508176930 (library bound) | ISBN 9781508178521 (paperback)
Subjects: LCSH: Sexism—Juvenile literature. | Misogyny—Juvenile literature.
Classification: LCC HQ1237 .A33 2017 | DDC 305.3—dc23
LC record available at https://lccn.loc.gov/2017018517

Manufactured in China

CONTENTS

Introduction 4

CHAPTER ONE
Running Like a Girl: The Influence of Sexism
and Misogyny on Individuals and Society 8

CHAPTER TWO
Flaws and Failings in Familiar Spaces: Sexism
and Misogyny in the Family, Relationships,
and School 28

CHAPTER THREE
In the Company of Strangers: Sexism
and Misogyny at Work, in Public Spaces,
and on College Campuses 45

CHAPTER FOUR
A Whole New (Digital) World: Sexism
and Misogyny on Social Media 65

CHAPTER FIVE
Can You Hear Me Now? Standing for
Change in a Sexist Society 83

GLOSSARY 96
FOR MORE INFORMATION 98
FOR FURTHER READING 104
BIBLIOGRAPHY...106
INDEX 109

INTRODUCTION

Perhaps the best reason to confront sexism is that it is the single most effective tool we have if we want to get rid of it. Hundreds of studies show that confronting bias (toward any group) actually improves intergroup perceptions and reduces future bias.

—Heidi Grant Halvorson, psychologist

Some say sexism is a term that is outdated and that it doesn't exist. The belief is that we now live in a "postfeminist" era, in which women and men have achieved equality. But consider the following examples:

- A girl is sent home for a dress code violation, while a boy is simply told to pull up his pants.
- A transgender boy is not allowed to use the boy's restroom.
- A girl working after school at a restaurant is paid less money for the same job as a boy.
- A girl is told by her friends that a sexist remark from a boy is a compliment because he's popular.
- A boy playing soccer is told to do better and "stop playing like a girl."

High school junior Elizabeth Skerry displays the poster she presented to the school board protesting the new school dress code.

- A boy calls a girl a prude because she won't sext; if she does, he calls her a slut.
- A girl is told she's too pretty to be smart. A boy can be smart no matter what he looks like.

- A boy gets hate tweets for calling out sexist jokes about a girl at school.

The aforementioned incidents are clearly examples of sexism in society; it still exists, but we often don't admit it or even respond to it. Many sexist practices have become so normalized that we accept them as part of our lives.

Consider some of the derogatory words and clichés that have become part of our language: "chick flick," "sissy bar," "bitchy," "dumb blonde." Boys are told not to "let a girl beat you" or "not to cry like a girl." A girl's a "slut," a guy's a "stud."

Sexism is not the same as sexual harassment. Sexism is the basis of the problem, the ideology that one gender is superior to the other, the root of prejudice from which harassment grows. Sexism is bias; sexual harassment is behavior that reflects sexist bias.

Sexism can mean not having equal opportunities or being treated as less competent. It rears its ugly head in double-standard policies made by schools, universities, and workplaces. It's all over social media. It's usually targeted at girls and transgender people, but boys can also be the victims of sexism.

Misogyny takes sexism a step further into actual hatred and extreme discrimination against women. It is thought to result from learning about sex and attitudes toward and treatment of women from sources that demean and diminish women and see them only as objects to be controlled by men.

Coping with sexism and misogyny requires that it is first recognized, then understood, and finally confronted and exposed. Only then can steps be taken toward counteracting its deleterious, or toxic, effects not only on girls and women, but also on boys, men, and transgender people.

CHAPTER ONE

Running Like a Girl: The Influence of Sexism and Misogyny on Individuals and Society

Honestly, I hate when in books, the guy changes the girl's life. Like, no. The girl needs to change her own life.

—Sasha Alsberg, writer

There is a T-shirt you can buy that says, "I Run like a Girl; Try to Keep Up." It's an effort to empower girls and counteract the commonly heard saying by boys, "you run like a girl," spoken as an insult to other boys whom they perceive as weak or underperforming. Other clichés, such as "you throw like a girl" or "go make me a sandwich," have become part of our language. Yet they both carry derogatory, sexist connotations.

Spotting Sexism

What exactly is sexism? Merriam-Webster's Dictionary defines sexism as:
- prejudice or discrimination based on sex, especially discrimination against women
- behavior, conditions, or attitudes that foster stereotypes of social roles based on sex

No matter what you call it, discrimination against both women and men is still pervasive, or widespread, in our society. But not everyone is aware of it. It's more than what people do; it's about the prejudices that they've learned from a young age that spill over into sexist behavior. You may make sexist remarks or be talked to in a sexist way and think that it's not a big deal. But it may be affecting you in ways you don't realize.

One college student's take on it is that sexist remarks and jokes aimed at girls are offensive because girls can relate to them; they feel personal. Guys can't relate if it's about girls, so they don't understand that it's offensive.

Sexism is not just directed at girls. It affects boys as well. They are generally expected to be strong, tough, aggressive, and unemotional. But if they aren't, they are often teased or harassed or told not to act "like a girl."

Sexism is often described as either hostile or benevolent. Hostile sexism is easy to spot. Someone

Sexism often targets transgender teens in gender-specific spaces like restrooms. However, some public places are beginning to relabel their restrooms as unisex.

yells insults, catcalls, or suggestive comments at you because you're a girl, whether you were assigned female at birth or are a transgender girl. You're blatantly told you're not as good or smart as a boy. If you are a transgender girl or boy, you might not be allowed in "women-only" or "men-only" spaces, such as restrooms or locker rooms.

Benevolent sexism can be subtler. It often sounds like a compliment, for example, "You're much too pretty to even think about becoming an engineer." It's patronizing, demoralizing, and insulting. It implies that women are dependent on men, weak and less intelligent or incompetent. It's a form of denial that women are still being discriminated against. But the discrimination is there.

Girls sometimes don't think sexism exists because the word is not used very often or is associated with being a "feminist." Feminism began in the 1800s in America with the movement to win women the right

Actor Emma Watson, who famously starred as the strong-willed and smart Hermione Granger in the Harry Potter films, is proud to call herself a feminist.

to vote. Then, in the 1960s and 1970s, it was perceived as a radical, man-hating movement in which women burned their bras and marched in protest parades. This association has kept a lot of girls from wanting to be called a feminist. Yet, today, many famous women, like Emma Watson, Beyoncé, and Geena Davis, are standing up and declaring that feminism is not about hating, it's a positive stand about achieving equality and fighting sexism.

Educating people about feminism may be one answer. An Ohio high school girl relates a class exercise in which both boys and girls were asked to stand behind a line. When the teacher read various statements, those who agreed stepped over the line. One of the statements was, "I am a feminist." Most of the girls stepped over, but hardly any boys. When they returned to class, the girl asked the teacher to explain what a feminist was. When she read the definition (someone who wants equality for women and men on social, political, economic, and legal levels) and asked again who would step over the line, every student raised his or her hand.

Perhaps the biggest issue that has to be fought is the fact that most sexism is not recognized as such. Clichés like "you throw like a girl" have become so much a part of our language that we may not even realize we are keeping sexism alive ourselves.

Am I Being Sexist? Six Questions to Ask Yourself

1. Do I use derogatory words to refer to girls, even if I'm a girl?
2. Do I tell guys they're acting "like a girl" if I think they're scared or weak or incompetent?
3. Do I trash transgender people?
4. Do I support music and videos by recording artists who objectify and disrespect women?
5. Do I think sexist jokes or demeaning pictures on social media are okay because "boys will be boys"?
6. If I get mad at a girl and dislike her, would I still dislike her for what she did if she were a boy?

Boys are not the only sexists; girls can act sexist, too.

In addition, if teens don't feel like they belong and have some sort of control over their lives, it often spews out in angry, sexist behavior. If you're a victim of this, don't try to handle it by yourself. Let others know what's going on; tell a parent, a teacher, or school guidance counselor.

Strategy Session: Think About Sexism

- Hang out with girls or boys who feel the same way you do about sexist words and other forms of discrimination against women. Together, tell other kids how you feel. If the situation makes you feel depressed or suicidal, get help from parents or a doctor.
- Ask to do a report about gender inequality for one of your classes; that way, it's the research speaking, not just your opinion.
- Ask school administrators about establishing workshops in school to educate everyone and provide open communication about the effects of sexism and inequalities in treatment between genders at school.

Why Do You Hate Me?

Hate is a harsh word, but it is the major component of the definition of misogyny: hatred, dislike, or mistrust of women, or prejudice against women. Theorists Peter

Glick and Susan Fiske describe it as "antagonism toward women who challenge men's power." It often manifests in domination of and discrimination against women. Men often don't realize they are misogynists. And men are not the only misogynists. Women sometimes hate or want to control other women, too.

According to Kate Manne in her article "The Logic of Misogyny," for the *Boston Review,* "Misogyny is what happens when women break ranks or roles and disrupt the patriarchal order: they tend to be perceived as uppity, unruly, out of line, or insubordinate. ... Misogyny isn't simply hateful; it imposes social costs on noncompliant women, who are liable to be labeled witches, bitches, sluts, and 'feminazis,' among other things." This plays out in most arenas: high schools, university campuses, workplaces, politics, and, most of all, social media.

In an article from YCteen, "Challenging Misogyny—Inside and Out," a high school girl talks about her choice of misogyny as the subject of a school paper assignment. What she learned surprised her. When she paid close attention to the song lyrics she listened to, she found many of them treated women with disrespect and as objects to be used and discarded. Many of her classmates agreed and were surprised, too. She also realized that the names girls sometimes called each other, like "bitch" or "ho," were really offensive. "Words have power; it's not okay to joke around using language that degrades women. We don't want men to do it, so why do we do it to each other?" Her decision after writing this paper was to change the way she talked to her girlfriends and to not let boys talk to her disrespectfully.

How to Spot a Misogynist

According to psychiatrist Dr. Berit Brogaard, most misogynists don't realize they hate women. It's "typically an unconscious hatred that men form early in life, often as a result of a trauma involving a female figure they trusted." Here are some typical traits of a misogynist, whether male, female, or transgender:

- His/her behavior is arrogant and self-centered; he/she wants to have control over women.
- He/she is extremely competitive with women.
- He/she doesn't keep his/her promises to women.
- On a date, he/she will treat a woman the opposite way that she prefers.
- He/she will cheat on a girlfriend.
- He/she will feel good about treating women badly.

Many boys are influenced by advertisements and social media into believing they have to be strong, powerful, and hide any sensitivity or vulnerability. These kinds of expectations often result in misogynistic behavior and can cross the line into sexual harassment and violence against women.

Transgender teens and adults struggle even more against misogyny. According to an article on USA Today Network, "there are more misconceptions, stereotypes and more hatred aimed at transgender women than transgender men."

Strategy Session: Think About Misogyny

- If someone makes misogynistic remarks, tell that person that it is disrespectful to you and that you don't want him or her to talk to you that way.
- Recognize and avoid misogynists if possible, especially when it comes to dating.
- Don't support music that objectifies women; write to the recording companies and let them know you won't buy any of their music and why.

Barbie Dolls, Bras, and Bulimia

Walk past the toy aisles in almost any store and you can spot the girl-centric aisle right away—everything is pink. Baby dolls, castles, toy kitchens, and princess-themed items make up the bulk of what is sold. Girls are told from an early age what girls are supposed to be like by the toys they play with, the clothes they wear, and the role models on television and in movies. The same can be said for boys. Their aisle is filled with cars, superheroes, tools, and science-related toys. Their role models are often muscle-bound cops, scientists, doctors, athletes, soldiers, and heads of corporations. And while girls have many more opportunities now as far as occupations (with a few exceptions), they are still being told that looking pretty is the most important thing to which they should aspire.

From Barbie dolls, to Disney princesses, to television and social media, girls get the message that the most important thing is to be thin, sexy, and beautiful. Sexualization is a form of discrimination. It happens when girls are objectified, when their value is considered to come only from their sexual appeal and physical appearance, to the exclusion of everything else. It begins at an early age, from stores that sell padded bras and thongs for seven-year-olds to preschool beauty pageants. On television and other media, girls are constantly reminded that they need to look sexy for boys and only have worth if they are beautiful. Yet, fewer than 5 percent of American women have bodies that look like the types seen in advertising (or the Disney princesses.)

Sexualization of girls begins at an early age. Advertisements, other media, and toys, such as Barbie, show an idealized yet unrealistic body image.

A report from the American Psychological Association found that "girls exposed to sexualized images from a young age are more prone to depression, eating disorders, and low self-esteem."

One teen says her friends worry about their weight all the time because the "girls on the Internet are perfect—amazing boobs, amazing figures, legs, everything and the girls know the guys talk about it and I guess they want to please the guys." In the United States alone, the cosmetics industry is a multibillion-dollar industry.

According to research through the Girls Scouts Research Institute, "60 percent of girls age thirteen to seventeen say they compare their bodies to fashion models." A 2013 High School Youth Risk Behavior Survey found that 63 percent of the girls in the study were trying to lose weight.

On Laura Bates's Everyday Sexism website, a fifteen-year-old girl posted, "I know I am smart, I know I am kind and funny, and I know that everybody around me keeps telling me that I can be whatever I want to be. I know all this, but I just don't feel that way. I always feel like if I don't look a certain way, if boys don't think I'm "sexy" or "hot" then I've failed and it doesn't even matter if I am a doctor or writer, I'll still feel like nothing."

Girls Can Make a Difference

Can one girl make a difference? Just ask Julia Bluhm. After fourteen-year-old Julia launched a protest to demand that more realistic pictures of girls and women be portrayed in the popular *Seventeen* magazine, the policies about retouching images were changed. Her petition, called Seventeen Magazine: Give Girls Images of Real Girls! garnered, or collected, eighty-four thousand signatures. A live, sign-holding protest was also held outside the magazine's New York offices.

Julia commented that the retouched images *Seventeen* uses "have a big effect on girls and their body image and how they feel about themselves." She thought that girls needed to see themselves represented more realistically.

Activist Julia Bluhm (*center*), with Spark Team members Izzy Labbe (*left*) and Maya Brown (*right*), petitioned *Seventeen* to show more realistic models in their magazine.

Media Mania and Me

Almost everywhere in their daily lives, girls are being portrayed as objects; they are constantly stared at, judged, criticized, and held up to a perfect standard that barely even exists. Easily accessed pornography and violent video games portray misogyny in action. This has created a confusing world for the average teen today and, for girls in particular, it is affecting teens' confidence, self-esteem, and health.

In many ways, a cisgender girl or transgender girl is at the mercy of what the media says she should look like and who she is supposed to be. According to the Media Education Foundation, "The average American is exposed to over 3,000 ads every single day and will spend two years of his or her life watching television commercials."

Male standards, as portrayed in films and games, can also be intimidating or perplexing. In her book *Everyday Sexism*, Laura Bates reveals these startling statistics about men: 63 percent of men think their arms or chests are not muscular enough. More than 1 in 10 men said they would trade a year of their life for the ideal body weight and shape. In the past three decades, male body image concerns have increased from 15 percent to 43 percent of men being dissatisfied with their bodies.

On many TV shows, girls are often portrayed as catty, bitchy, mean, or trashy. According to Dr. Charisse Nixon, a developmental psychologist, "We are inundated with media images of cruel behavior as funny . . . with reality television shows that celebrate meanness."

The best thing you can do is learn more about and be aware of how media is affecting you. Consider getting involved in movements like SPARK, an organization working for gender justice for girls, or the Dove Self-Esteem Project, which works to promote body confidence for girls all over the world. The 4 Every Girl website is challenging the media industry to show

Dove's Self-Esteem Project strives to boost girls' body confidence because "anxiety over appearance keeps girls from being their best selves."

more positive, healthy images of girls. The site has a whole section on what you can do to get involved.

Strategy Session: Think About Media Influences

- Realize that what you look like is only one part of your life. Don't allow others to define you or tell you what you have to look like or that you have to be perfect.
- Join an organization that empowers girls and works for change, such as SPARK, Girls Action Foundation in Canada, or Feminist.com in the United States.
- If you are experiencing depression or an eating disorder, get help from parents, counselors, and physicians.

Myths & FACTS

Myth: The definition of a feminist is a woman who hates men.

Fact: Feminists can be men, too. The actual definition is a person who advocates for social, economic, legal, and political rights for women equal to those of men.

Myth: Men and women are equal now, at least in the United States and Canada.

Fact: Women in both countries are paid less than men for the same jobs, are unequally represented in government, and still hold very few of the highest corporate business positions. In the United States, women will not have total protection under the law until the Equal Rights Amendment is passed.

Myth: There's nothing teens can do to change sexism at school, work, or on social media..

Fact: There are many people and organizations that are fighting sexism in all those arenas. Teens can get involved and try to effect change.

CHAPTER TWO

Flaws and Failings in Familiar Spaces: Sexism and Misogyny in the Family, Relationships, and School

"**H**ow good does a female athlete have to be before we just call her an athlete?" The author of this quote is unknown, but the words ring all too true. Sexism and misogyny present themselves in many ways within familiar dynamics, such as family, school, and dating.

All in the Family

According to research from Marquette University, "Sexism can be perpetuated in our homes by the ones we love." They probably don't recognize actions as being sexist or intentionally continue them, but they do have an effect on teens' perception of what role they play within the

Roles people play in their families are often filled according to gender and tradition instead of genuine interest or passion.

family unit and what is expected of them. Parents may reward daughters for excelling in traditional female roles, such as housekeeping and cooking, while discouraging them from helping fix the car or learning how to do carpentry. The same goes for boys, only in reverse. These actions can perpetuate sexist roles and expectations.

How parents treat each other and what their roles are within the family influence how teens decide how they should act. Often, the mother juggles work outside the home as well as most of the running of the household, while the father doesn't contribute anything more than his income from his job. Conversely, many parents make an effort to divide responsibilities equally.

Your perceptions of gender roles will likely be greatly influenced by the people who are raising you. They may even be unaware of gender inequalities, of treating boys better than girls or vice versa or of influencing your choice of career or extracurricular activities, but it would be unusual if they didn't.

Think about your role within your family. What do you talk about? What responsibilities do you have? How do you talk to one another? What things are your parents teaching you for when you leave home and establish your own place?

You can't change who the people in your family are, and you may be happy with the status quo. If not, Hera Cook, a historian of feminism, women, and sexuality, has some solid advice for coping and/or effecting change. "Basically," she says, "you can't ask your family members to change how they live. You can only share ideas, and there are few easy ways to share ideas that challenge people's everyday behavior." Cook suggests asking to share tasks you have to do more equally among your siblings if that is an issue or switching them around, so that no one is only doing chores that are traditionally malecentric or femalecentric.

Maybe you have a brother or other relative who uses derogatory, sexist words about girls. Ask how he would feel if someone called him something derogatory.

Another thing Cook suggests is what she calls "reflective listening." People tend to talk passionately

Coping with sexist attitudes within the family can be challenging. You can't change who a person is, but you can still share ideas and have discussions about behavior.

about an issue about which they believe they are right. She says, "We are so keen to get our own point of view across, we rarely listen to the other. But I think this may be a powerful tool for you. Let your family explain their thinking and ask them questions about it: this is a great way to get people to think about their behavior without telling them to change it."

Your parents or siblings may see sexist attitudes and language differently from you, but ultimately you have control only over your own attitudes and language. If you are more aware of what you are saying and how it is affecting those around you, you can decide what kind of person you want to be, within the family and outside of it. That's all up to you.

Classrooms, Comments, and Complaints

In a Canadian high school where both boys and girls were interviewed, the terms "sexism" and "feminism" were considered outdated. The word "sexism" isn't used very often. But both boys and girls admitted that they saw a lot of inequalities because of gender, and one girl said that women and men should be treated equally, but she didn't see that they were. Inequality and sexism exist, but they are not often called out.

In her book, *Gender, Bullying and Harassment: Strategies to End Sexism and Homophobia in Schools,*

Elizabeth J. Meyer feels that change can happen only if a shift in the school culture happens. School leadership is a key factor in creating and sustaining the culture of the school. She feels what might help is for administrators and teachers to respond more to complaints and revise policies to address some of the following issues: sexist jokes and comments, double standards in dress codes and sports, and issues affecting transgender teens.

Sexist jokes and comments are part of the culture, not just in high school, but just about everywhere. Many girls are offended but often ignore them because they are embarrassed or because of peer pressure; they don't want to stand out or be thought of as different. Boys don't think girls should take them too seriously. One boy interviewed in the book *Smart Girls*, by Shauna Pomerantz and Rebecca Raby, acknowledged that sexist jokes might make girls feel bad but felt that it was *their* problem because the girls should have thicker skins.

According to the National Organization for Women (NOW), "When schools ... ignore sexist behavior in the classroom, they give tacit approval to those kinds of behaviors. When there is a lack of attempt to discipline boys for harassing female students, it perpetuates the idea that it's the girl's responsibility to protect herself from feeling unsafe."

The more sexist jokes and slurs are seen as acceptable, the more a school culture encourages the idea that it's okay to put women down. According to her article titled "No Kidding: Sexist Jokes Aren't Funny, They're Hostile," Toula Drimonis states, "A research project led by a Western Carolina University psychology professor indicates that exposure to sexist humor can lead to tolerance of hostile feelings and discrimination against women."

Jocks and Jills

Another area where double standards and gender inequality exists is in sports. One group of Canadian girls complained that boys (playing hockey) usually got better rink time, more expensive uniforms, larger audiences, and more administrative support.

In her article "Defeating Sexism in Sports Culture," Ashley Lauren Samsa writes, "Some girls who love sports and have competed their whole lives refuse to try out once they get to high school because, in high school, reputation is everything and they don't want to pigeonhole themselves as jocks." Athletic girls might still have to deal with pervasive sexism in sports but many of them are joining sports teams anyway. Samsa sees it as a way for girls to change negative stereotypes of women by simply refusing to follow them. "These changes are happening within a firmly entrenched male-dominated athletic universe, and the students behind them need support."

Because participation was determined by birth certificate sex, transgender teen Mack Beggs had to compete on the girls' wrestling team.

In the United States, Title IX protects students from discrimination based on sex in education programs or activities that receive federal financial assistance. While sports is covered as an activity, it doesn't mean that girls are required to be allowed to play on the same sports teams with boys, merely that they are to be given equal opportunities to play sports. Title IX states that "Title IX does not require institutions to offer identical sports, but an equal opportunity to play."

Decades of stereotypes and expectations are never changed overnight. But, looking at the sports culture in new ways can be a possible avenue for change. According to an article in Teen Ink by Hannah S. Ardsley, "The decision for teams shouldn't be sex; it should be skill. Any girl should be allowed on any team if she has the necessary skills."

I Have to Wear WHAT?

Sexism in school dress codes is another source of controversy in many schools across the United States and Canada. Students are protesting the codes, claiming that they are unequal between genders and noninclusive to transgender students. The reason often given for disallowing inappropriate dress for girls is that it is too distracting to boys. Yet this sends a message that boys are incapable of being responsible for their own actions and the fault lies with the girls.

According to Shauna Pomerantz, a Brock University associate professor of child and youth studies, "Constantly asking girls to cover up creates a society where young boys don't know how to treat girls. ... The more people project that image on them, the more they adopt it. Boys are never being asked to think about how they look at, judge and demean girls."

Transgender students have also been targeted; some have been sent home for wearing clothing considered to be different from what's expected of their legal sex.

A teen girl, when asked about gender inequality in her high school dress codes, said that she felt boys and girls were treated equally when it came to violations, with one exception: the football team members. They suffered no consequences for violating the dress code. Most of the student body objected and took the issue to the administration.

Dress code violators are often made to wear special clothes that loudly proclaim to the entire school that they have violated the dress code. Many students and parents feel that this is a form of shaming. For example, a high school in Ohio makes teens wear what they call "Spare Attire," a sweat suit that has tire tracks stenciled across it, to cover dress code violations. One student said she has never seen any boys made to wear the suit, only girls.

Shown here is one girl's protest against "a distraction for boys" being used as the reason for the parameters of her high school's dress code for girls.

Protest by Switch

The dress code of a California school stated that boys could not wear long hair or earrings to school. To protest, a group of boys wore dresses to school and girls wore men's button-down shirts. "The reason we switched gender norms for the day was to make a statement that what we wear does not define us," student Emma Sledd told the *Fresno Bee*. "Our district school code should not favor or discriminate any gender. We believe everyone should be able to express themselves equally. A boy with long hair is no less of a hard worker than a girl with long hair."

Lydia Cleveland, a Virginia teen, decided to do something about a similar situation at her high school. She wrote a letter to the school administrators, asking them to stop making dress code violators wear a sweat suit with the words "Dress Code" written on it. In an interview with MTV news, Cleveland said this practice is "telling young women: 'It's your responsibility to cover up. You are a distraction. This is your problem.' And we're simultaneously telling young men, 'This isn't your problem. If you're distracted, it's all girls' fault—you can't help it.'"

Strategy Session: Dealing with Dress Codes and More in the Classroom

- If you feel that the dress codes at your school are unfair or targeted mostly at girls, talk to your parents about going to the school administration and asking for a reevaluation of their policies.
- If you find sexist jokes and slurs offensive, tell the person who said it that it's offensive to you but without getting angry or upset at him or her. If you can get a group of other students together who feel like you do, it will have more power.
- Work to get codes of conduct posted and enforced.
- If you are being treated unfairly in the classroom, either by boys, girls, or your teachers, talk to

your parents or school counselor about getting help dealing with the problem and how it is affecting you.

Because My Partner Says So

Dating is probably one area where sexism can be extremely overt and difficult to deal with because it's all tied into your emotions. Hearing sexist jokes or being the target of sexist slurs is hard enough to take from guys or girls with whom you aren't friends. But when it comes from someone you really care about, it's often hard to know what to do.

Relationships tend to fall into something called gender profiling, a term that means boys and girls have preconceived ideas of the roles each is supposed to play, based only on gender. For example, in traditional heterosexual dating scenarios, boys still are expected to take the lead as far as asking a girl out, picking her up, paying for a meal, etc. In addition, they often decide whether or not a relationship is going to be serious.

Generally, girls have been taught that asking guys out is perceived as pushy and even masculine, that it means you're desperate for a date, that it's not sexy, and that it emasculates, or weakens, boys. Erin Tatum, a contributing writer for Everyday Feminism, argues that a lot of these ideas are outdated. "Pursuing your desires is never a bad thing, and you shouldn't

A lot of teens decide not to follow what they consider to be outdated gender-based roles and expectations in their dating lives.

apologize for it. If you want that guy, go out there and get him—or at least ask him if he's interested. No one should shame you for making a move."

While dating dynamics may be changing, how you treat each other while dating is a whole different issue altogether.

Is Your Date Sexist?

How does your boyfriend or girlfriend talk to you?
- Does he or she compliment you by comparing you to other girls?
- Does he or she interrupt you frequently?
- Does he or she belittle you?
- Does he or she insist on physical intimacy without asking for your consent?
- Does he or she make gender-based assumptions about you instead of wanting to know what you really think or feel? (For example, you're a woman, you must like kids.)
- Does he or she make sexist jokes at your expense?
- Does he or she always want to make all of the decisions?
- Does he or she give you a hard time for bringing any issues related to the above questions up?

Also pay attention to how your partner lets others talk to or about you. One Twitter user shared that her boyfriend's friend said to him (about her), "I see you hitting that." Her response was, "This may not seem like a big deal to some of you, but I felt sick and objectified. Things like this happen all the time and are the kinds of moments that contribute to women's sense of fear and inadequacy. I am not a piece of meat that a man gets to utilize for his pleasure. It hurts my heart that so many young people are so comfortable…using these phrases and objectifying women with such ease."

Strategy Session: On a Date

- Go on a double date or go out with a new date in groups before you go out with someone alone; it's a good way to get to know someone first.
- Make sure your date is someone to whom you can talk about how you want to be treated.
- If he makes sexist remarks to his friends about you, tell him it bothers you, and ask him to stop.
- Make sure your date understands consent and where you stand.
- Learn self-defense in case he or she tries to push you beyond your line of consent.
- Talk to an adult if you are in a situation you don't feel you can control.

In the Company of Strangers: Sexism and Misogyny at Work, in Public Spaces, and on College Campuses

The test for whether or not you can hold a job should not be the arrangement of your chromosomes.

— Bella Abzug, lawyer and activist

As a teen, you may not have a job yet, or you may have an after-school or summer job. But chances are, if you aren't working now, you will be soon, either right after high school, college, or another type of training. Chances are also, especially as a girl, that you either have encountered or will encounter sexism at your place of work.

Shown here is Bella Abzug, women's rights activist.

Similarly, very few girls and women have not been the victim of catcalling or other forms of sexual harassment in public spaces, such as in restaurants, on public transportation, and walking home from school or jogging in the park. It happens in many places, including on college campuses, where teens are often on their own for the first time and living with or attending classes with people from many different backgrounds and cultures. Finding ways to cope with diverse situations can be challenging.

It's Off to Work I Go

According to Melanie C. Steffens and Maria Angels Viladot, there are ingrained cultural perceptions of women that affect how they are treated in the workplace. Women are seen as either "traditional" (housewife), "modern" (nontraditional), or "sensual" (sexy). These perceptions color the way women are treated in the workplace. Sexist attitudes, if

47

deeply ingrained in a culture, often keep women from advancing into better-paying positions and becoming successful and fulfilled in their careers.

Jacqueline Yi, in a psychology research paper, blames benevolent sexist stereotypes for some of the issues encountered in the workplace. "Men are … viewed as highly competent, and therefore, well-suited for high-status workplace positions (Glick & Fiske, 2001). In contrast, women are assigned communal stereotypes, such as having nurturing, interdependent, and considerate characteristics, which are suitable for the duties of a proper wife and mother (Good & Sanchez, 2009). While these domestic roles are important to society, they enforce the idea that women are subservient to men, as well as incompetent and incapable without their financial support."

Bias is not always conscious, but the results can be unfair. In a study by scientists at Yale University, applications for science-based jobs were sent to research universities. Some applications had male names and some had female names. "The study revealed that recruiters (both male and female) rated the 'male' applicants as 'significantly more competent and hirable' than the identical 'female' applicants. They also offered the 'males' higher salaries." These stereotypes play out as factors that can impede women from procuring a job or wanting to stay at one in which they feel they are being discriminated against on the basis of gender.

Women are often the victims of sexist attitudes and gender bias during job interviews. They may not get a job for which they are qualified based on their gender.

I'm Smarter Than You Think I Look

Appearance is another factor that often dominates decisions on how women are treated at work. Girls who are considered pretty often receive better treatment. Sometimes, however, if your outfit is very feminine or sexy, people may think you are not as smart as their male counterpart.

Women are frequently "rated" according to their looks and treated differently because of how they look. According to an article from Buzzfeed, "9 Stories of Everyday Sexism," a waitress, while at her job one day, observed a cute college girl come in to drop off a job application. After she left, the waitress heard the head bartender say, "She's an 8. I'll call her tomorrow." They didn't check her work experience or references. Another woman who came in (with excellent experience) was considered a "5" and wasn't hired. The "8" turned out to be a terrible waitress. In another instance, a dental assistant, who had ten years of exemplary service, was fired for being "too sexy." She filed a gender discrimination suit that went through several courts, but she ultimately lost the suit.

Girls today are being told that they can grow up to be anything they want to be. And for many girls, it's true. But once girls get into the job market, the reality often undermines the myth of equality.

Worth Less

Unequal pay at work is one of the most blatant and pervasive examples of sexism. In their book *Smart Girls*, Shauna Pomerantz and Rebecca Raby point out that, "While educational opportunities for women have expanded rapidly, work cultures have been slow to change." And even though many girls excel in school, "this success does not translate into a transformation of power at the highest levels and economic inequality stubbornly endures."

According to statistics in Everyday Sexism, in the United States, women are paid 82 percent of what their male counterparts make just one year after college graduation. Overall, women only earn about 78 percent of what men earn. Among financial managers, the percentage drops to around 70 percent.

A study by Hired, a jobs site, found that, overall, women are getting paid between 3 percent and 30 percent less than their male counterparts in the fields of technology, sales, and marketing. Jessica Kirkpatrick, author of the study, said, "It's difficult to determine whether this is a symptom of unconscious gender bias in the hiring process or results from an ongoing cycle of women being underpaid, setting their salary expectations too low, and ultimately receiving less in subsequent roles."

Don't be afraid to ask for a better salary; studies show that if you ask for it, you just might get it.

But the news is not all bad. The study also found that one group of women with fewer than two years' experience actually got 7 percent more than equally inexperienced men in the same career fields. The reason? They asked. According to Kirkpatrick, "Women who ask for the same salary as men in the same role tend to get offers in line with what they are asking."

Just Out of Reach

Achieving high-level jobs, what Pomerantz and Raby call "power at the highest levels," is often never realized for many women. According to an article in Business Insider, research by LeanIn.org and McKinley & Co. found that "women are a whopping 15 percent less likely than men to get promoted. The researchers say that, at this rate, it will take more than a century to achieve gender parity." The study further shows, "Women were nearly three times more likely than men to say their gender has posed a hindrance to their career advancement. They also said that they're consulted less often on key decisions."

Statistics reflect the gender gap. According to a 2016 report, *Statistical Overview of Women in the Workforce,* in Canada, "men are two to three times more likely to be in a senior management position than are women." Only one-third of Canadian women hold senior management positions. In the United States, women hold 51.5 percent of management and professional positions, but only 4 percent of CEO positions in S&P 500 companies.

How does this affect women? A study by researchers at the University of Melbourne found that sexist jokes, questioning women's competencies, lower pay, and fewer opportunities for advancement, all examples of "low-level sexism," could have serious psychological consequences. "Our results suggest that organizations should have zero tolerance for low-intensity sexism the same way they do for overt harassment."

So Says Beyoncé

Beyoncé Giselle Knowles-Carter is a famous singer, songwriter, and actor. "Women have to work much harder to make it in this world," she says. "It really pisses me off that women don't get the same opportunities as men, or money, for that matter. Because, let's face it, money gives men the power to run the show. It gives men the power to define our values, and to define what's sexy, and what's feminine."

Beyoncé is just one celebrity who speaks out against women getting fewer opportunities as well as lower salaries and less power than men.

Beyoncé has joined with other entertainers and world leaders in a girl empowerment campaign called Ban Bossy. In a *People* article, she says, "Girls are less interested in leadership than boys…and that's because they worry about being called 'bossy' while little boys who step up are called 'leaders'."

Girls have many more opportunities today than they ever have. Though there are still a lot of sexist attitudes and behavior in the workplace, not all women encounter them. In addition, many companies, organizations, and politicians are working on ways to help more women achieve their dreams.

Strategy Session: Sexism at Work

- When you start a new job, learn what your rights are and what is allowed and not allowed or supported.
- If you and your coworkers have been treated unfairly because of gender, get together and agree to stand up for one another.
- Document any unwanted advances and tell someone else about them.
- Try not to be alone with someone who has made sexist remarks to you.
- In a job interview, describe yourself with words like "independent," "confident," and "fair" instead of "kind," "helpful," or "sympathetic."
- If there is a union where you work, find out if they can help in cases of gender discrimination.

Gropes, Grabs, and Catcalls

Public spaces, such as restaurants, stores, public transportation, and streets, are places where sexism proliferates, or thrives. It's so much a part of so many people's lives that it's becoming normalized. Of course, it isn't just women who are the victims; boys also experience sexism in public places. But the majority who experience it are still cisgender and transgender girls and women.

A 2014 survey by an organization called Stop Street Harassment (SSH) found that 65 percent of all women had experienced some form of street harassment, compared to 25 percent of men. Transgender individuals face even higher rates of public discrimination.

According to Laura Bates, founder of The Everyday Sexism Project, more than ten thousand women have reported to the website that they have experienced sexism and harassment in public spaces. One mother of a fourteen-year-old girl says that her daughter "gets cat-called and whistled at so often walking to school that she thinks it's just part of life."

But it shouldn't be. The effects of this can be far-reaching. Allowing the seemingly "minor" name-calling can lead to more serious harassment, abuse, and violence. It can negatively impact girls' self-esteem and perpetuates the mentality of victim blaming. It also creates an atmosphere of fear. Girls, far more than boys, have to be conscious of what they wear, be careful where they walk, what time of day they go places, and seek the safety of a group, which is not always possible.

A jaw-dropping 65 percent of women have experienced sexism in the form of street harassment, compared to only 25 percent of men. Those numbers increase for transgender individuals.

In her book *He's a Stud, She's a Slut and 49 Other Double Standards Every Woman Should Know,* Jessica Valenti says that "sexism has it so ingrained in men's minds (and even our own sometimes) that women are there to be looked at, commented on and grabbed that it's hard to imagine anything that would facilitate real change."

In some cities, rather than dealing with the harassers, segregated spaces (men only and women only) have been established. But Betsy Eudey, director of gender studies at California State University, contends, "segregated spaces only enhance division by sex and prevent necessary actions needed to make public spaces safe and welcoming to all."

Websites like Stop Street Harassment have a mission to effect change. They offer ideas of what kids and adults can do to stand up to everyday sexism in public places, as well as hosting an annual Anti-Street Harassment Week.

Strategy Session: Public Sexism

- Report to your parents or a counselor any incidents of sexism or misogyny you have experienced in a public place. Laura Bates says, "For every woman who manages to stand up and say no, there's another harasser who will think twice the next time."
- Try to walk in groups, if possible.
- Help raise awareness by sharing your story or encouraging a friend to share hers on sites like Everyday Sexism (www.everydaysexism .com) and Stop Street Harassment (www .stopstreetharassment.org). Students to whom this happens are not alone. Draw strength from others who have similar experiences.
- Don't accept it if people tell you not to make a fuss, to be glad for the attention, or that it's your fault. It's never okay to be treated disrespectfully.

Dorms, Dates, and Decisions: Sexism on College Campuses

The following scenarios are all too common, even in this day and age. A woman lands a scholarship to a prestigious law school and is asked whom she slept with to get it. A business professor tells a female student that women don't become millionaires, they marry millionaires. A female college student asks a physics professor if he would please write a formula out on the board. He replies that the request is not unexpected because women struggle with math more than men do. Sexism on college campuses is often blatant, especially in the classroom.

In an article titled "College Women Sound Off on the Disturbing Sexism They Face Every Day," women talk about the sexism encountered in their classrooms. One student related that, "In some of my male-dominated classes, I have noticed that male students tend to interrupt female students more than their male peers, and they mansplain basic concepts to them. … I once had a guy in one of my advanced government classes try to mansplain the structure of the American legislative system to me; that was pretty funny (and insulting)."

STEMwomen.net addresses issues that girls who want to go into the STEM (science, technology, engineering, and math) fields face: "The scientific literature has shown that there are inequalities between women and men in STEM. Denying that a problem exists is the single biggest obstacle in promoting gender equity in science."

If women assert themselves, they have to walk a fine line between being taken seriously and being thought of as "bitchy." Proving they are just as competent as the guys often mitigates the sexist

College women often experience sexist attitudes and condescending treatment, such as interruptions or "mansplaining," especially in male-dominated fields like STEM.

attitudes, though, and confronting the issue can sometimes raise awareness and resolve the problem.

In a study of 169 college women by Cheryl R. Kaiser and Carol T. Miller, "A Stress and Coping Perspective on Confronting Sexism," the results showed that, although confronting sexism is a viable, though sometimes difficult coping strategy, if women don't speak up, it appears as though they're okay with being discriminated against. But if it's acknowledged, it gives other women a forum for expressing dissatisfaction. This can lead to the formation of organizations and motivate people to start campaigns and actions that can effect change.

One such organization that is tackling the issue of gender discrimination is the Association of American University Women (AAUW). They are a 130-year-old, grassroots organization whose mission is to empower women in universities as individuals and as a community.

They offer a legal advocacy fund to challenge sex discrimination not only in the college classroom but also in the workplace. They support student-led, campus action projects that deal with discrimination and gender bias, especially in the STEM fields.

Umona Okorafor, an engineer and founder of a foundation called Working to Advance STEM Education for African Women (WAAW) says that both genders need to be included in trying to balance the number of men and women in STEM fields. "However, until everyone begins to see that empowering women empowers entire communities, there will be limits to improvement. Men need to understand the value of women and become advocates."

Strategy Session: Sexism on Campus

- Confront those who discriminate against you; they may be unaware that their remarks or attitudes are sexist and offensive.
- Demonstrate that you can do the work as well as or better than someone who thinks you can't do it as well as a man.
- Join with others in organizations like AAUW to challenge gender discrimination together.

A Whole New (Digital) World: Sexism and Misogyny on Social Media

I spoke to girls who said, 'social media is destroying our lives, ... but we can't go off it, because then we'd have no life.'

—**Nancy Jo Sales, author of *American Girls: Social Media and the Secret Lives of Teenagers***

Teens live on social media, mostly via their smartphones, and it has opened a new world of communication, knowledge, and expression. It's also turned out to be a vehicle for sexism and misogyny. In some ways, it's the ultimate arena for turning women into objects. Online, a woman can be treated as:

- A tool to be used
- Interchangeable with other objects
- Having no agency (the ability to take action or control your life)

Social media, which is used by teens all the time, offers ample opportunities for sexism and misogyny, with anonymous disparaging and objectifying posts and comments to and about women.

- Just a photo
- Just what she looks like
- Something that is owned
- Someone with no boundaries to keep her from being violated
- Someone whose feelings don't count
- Just a body part
- Someone who can't talk back

The anonymity of social media has afforded people the advantage of being able to channel reams of hate, bullying, and harassment at others without revealing their own identities. Most teens on social media platforms like Twitter, Facebook, Instagram, Snapchat, and others deal with some form of sexism or misogyny regularly. An article called "Sexism and Social Media: What It's Like to Be a Teenager Today" stated, "On a daily, sometimes hourly, basis, on their phones, they [teens] encounter things which are offensive and potentially damaging to their well-being and sense of self-esteem."

Some sites can be blatantly misogynistic, like sections on Reddit, whose members are 87 percent white, male, young, and wealthy. One moderator sees it as a place where men can vent, blow off steam, and try to understand women. Others view it as a toxic slice of the "manosphere," a network of websites and blogs dedicated to addressing men's issues.

In the article "How Social Media Is Disrupting the Lives of American Girls," Nancy Jo Sales writes, "One factor in sexualization that is too often ignored is the rise of online porn." Porn depicts sex in ways that objectify (mostly) women and often portray it in ways that are devoid of human emotion or real connections. Because it depicts a false view of what healthy sexual relationships look like, it widens the gap of understanding between genders and perpetuates gender-role stereotypes and sexist attitudes.

Peggy Orenstein, author of *Girls & Sex: Navigating the Complicated New Landscape,* says that, "By college, according to a survey of more than eight hundred students entitled 'Generation XXX,' 90 percent of men and a third of women had viewed porn during the preceding year...Even if what they watch is utterly vanilla, they're still learning that women's sexuality exists for the benefit of men."

Some social media sites offer tools to fight sexism and misogyny. On Facebook, Twitter, and others, you can unfriend or block a user, report the user to the administrators, and document and save an offensive post. Though many social media sites claim to prohibit certain postings, like nudity, that doesn't always happen. One recommendation is that you don't retaliate. Also, don't keep it a secret; tell someone you trust, like a parent, friend, or teacher. If you're really afraid, contact the police.

Sexist Words Used for Women

According to actress Jennifer Garner, "Words matter. When a little girl is called 'bossy' when she leads, it's telling her to be quiet. I don't want little girls to be quiet. I want them to roar."

Some sexist words about appearance, like "frumpy," "curvy," "mousy," "cheap," and "plus sized," are never used about men. Nor do people refer to men as having a "blonde" moment, inferring that they are dumb. Consider this short list of sexist words frequently used in reference to women:

- Bitch
- Slut (boys are studs)
- Prima donna
- Drama queen (boys are expressive)
- Abrasive
- Bossy (boys are powerful)
- Frigid
- Hormonal/Emotional (boys are passionate)
- Ditzy
- Nag (boys are persistent)
- Tramp

Reclaim the Internet is a movement dedicated to taking action by challenging abuse on social media. Jess Phillips, a British elected official and one of the founders of Reclaim the Internet, says the campaign "is trying to make sure that freedom of speech for all the amazing girls and women is not drowned out by faceless avatars. I want spunky women shouting up and facing honest to goodness debate and challenge. Not men with spunky names bullying women into silence."

Strategy Session: Online Tactics

- Document unwanted, inappropriate posts, then unfriend or block the user.
- Let others you trust know about any issues you're having with someone on social media.
- Report inappropriate posts to the social media site.
- If it escalates into cyberbullying or sexual harassment, report it to parents or the police.
- Get involved with the Reclaim the Internet campaign.

Jess Phillips, an elected British official, challenges abuse on social media through a movement she helped found called Reclaim the Internet.

The Trouble with Trolls

Trolls are online bullies who deliberately make offensive posts to upset others and get a response. They are usually self-absorbed, like to exaggerate, have poor spelling and grammar, and use ad-hominem attacks (attacking a person's character rather than answering an argument).

According to Joel Stein, a contributor to *Time*, "Internet trolls have a manifesto of sorts, which states they are doing it for the 'lulz,' or laughs. What trolls do for the lulz ranges from clever pranks to harassment to violent threats. ... When victims do not experience lulz, trolls tell them they have no sense of humor. Trolls are turning social media and comment boards into a giant locker room in a teen movie, with towel-snapping racial epithets and misogyny."

One example of trolling is when Olympic diver Tom Daley received a tweet from a troll on Twitter saying he let his father down by not winning the gold medal. Tom's father had recently

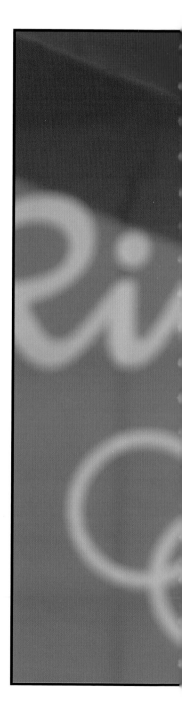

Tom Daley, an Olympic diver, was a victim of internet trolls, who targeted him with nasty comments about his recently deceased father.

died of cancer. Singer Gary Barlow was trolled with malicious tweets about his baby daughter who was stillborn.

In a 2016 article "Internet Trolling: Quarter of Teenagers Suffered Online Abuse Last Year," a survey of thirteen- to eighteen-year-olds found that "24 percent had been targeted due to their gender, sexual orientation, race, religion, disability or transgender identity. One in 25 said they were singled out for abuse all or most of the time."

The good news is that the majority of the teens say that their friends have been there for them with online support.

Will Gardner, chief executive of the charity Childnet, commented, "While it is encouraging to see that almost all young people believe no one should be targeted with online hate, and heartening to hear about the ways young people are using technology to take positive action online to empower each other and spread kindness, we were surprised and concerned to see that so many had been exposed to online hate in the last year."

Strategy Session: Dealing with Trolls

- Ignore them.
- Document what the troll says, then delete.

- Report them to Facebook, Twitter, or whatever site you are on.
- If you're online with others, address them and say, "We've got a troll; let's ignore him."
- Don't try to argue with a troll.
- Disable commenting from your posts, if appropriate.
- Fight back with facts if the troll is telling lies about you.
- Consider changing your profile to appear male if you are a girl.

If you continue to be bothered by trolls, and none of the above strategies work, tell your parents or a counselor. Don't try to deal with them by yourself. Troll behavior can escalate and become more invasive.

Victimology

In an article by Nina Burleigh in the *Observer*, Jackson Katz, creator of the MVP Playbooks, says, "There has been a dramatic desensitization to women's humanity and sexual agency through media representations that have become completely mainstream. It is more accessible, and the porn itself has gotten way more brutal. There is no question that the level of open misogyny and brutality in our culture has grown as well."

Screenwriter Jane Goldman (who wrote the screenplay for *Miss Peregrine's Home for Peculiar Children*) left Twitter because of social media abuse.

Many victims are celebrities, teachers, and politicians.

Some of the celebrities who've left Twitter over social media abuse include actresses Jennifer Lawrence (*Hunger Games*) and Lily James (*Cinderella* and *Downton Abbey*), actor Stephen Fry (*Alice Through the Looking Glass*), Zelda Williams (daughter of Robin Williams), screenwriter Jane Goldman (*Miss Peregrine's Home for Peculiar Children*), singers Tom Clarke and Sinead O'Connor, and comedian Matt Lucas.

According to an article by Sandra Laville, "Research Reveals Huge Scale of Social Media Misogyny," more than six hundred teachers had been harassed on social media in regard to their work, and many of those doing the harassing were parents. In the same article, a teacher reported that, "One parent threatened to smash my face in a post on Facebook."

For teens, being victims of sexism and misogyny on social media can have long-lasting effects. Charisse Nixon, a developmental psychologist, in a WebMD article, "Mean Girls: How to Deal With Them," explains the far-reaching effects of sexism on social media as opposed to a situation at school. "Being insulted or harassed at school is much different than being insulted or harassed online. At school, maybe a couple of other people could find out what happened. When something embarrassing is posted on your Facebook or Myspace page, hundreds or even thousands of people might see it."

Hate on High

Politicians have always been the victims of media scrutiny, but social media has taken exposure to a whole new level. According to an article by the International Knowledge Network of Women in Politics, "Modern technology, including emails, blogs and social media platforms, have supplied new avenues for circulating abusive content regarding women in general, and more specifically to women active in politics, as bloggers, activists or politicians."

Mike Crawley, CBC News, reported that Ontario premier Kathleen Wynne has suffered a barrage of hate tweets directed at her since her election in 2013. "The kinds of things we're seeing on social media undermine civility," Wynne said. "I think it discourages people from even entering politics." She is concerned that the reality of exposing oneself to this kind of abuse will discourage young women from running for office.

Ontario premier Kathleen Wynne (*right*) is concerned that the volume of hate tweets female politicians often endure could deter young women from running for political office.

The internet also gives mean girls, as well as mean guys, an easy way to hide. "We found that kids tend to think that because they're behind a screen they're not responsible—that they can say whatever they want," Nixon says. "What kids need to understand is that whenever they are on the screen, they leave a fingerprint. Nasty or humiliating comments posted today can stay online for years—even after they're deleted."

Strategy Session: Security Online

- Don't accept a friend request from a stranger.
- Use the security settings set up by your social media sites.
- Take action, like blocking, unfriending, and the like, right away.

10 Great Questions to Ask a Counselor

1. I feel upset when boys tell sexist jokes; how can I deal with that?

2. I want to do something about all the sexist stuff that goes on at school, but I don't want to be made fun of. How do I get over the fear of speaking up?

3. I'm really good at basketball but there's no girls' team at my school, and the school won't let me play on the basketball team. Can I do anything about that?

4. My boyfriend disrespects me in front of his friends. I don't want to break up; what can I do?

5. Our school dress code is unfair and seems to apply only to girls. Can I do anything about it?

6. The music my friends listen to puts women down. I don't like it, but I don't want to lose my friends. What should I do?

7. I found out the boys I work with, who do the same job as the girls, get paid more. Can I do anything about that?

(continued on the next page)

10 Great Questions to Ask a Counselor

(continued from the previous page)

8. My boyfriend is pressuring me to sext with him; I don't want to, but I don't want to break up with him. What should I do?

9. How can I stop somebody from spreading lies about me on Twitter?

10. I'm a transgender boy and was told I can't use the boys' bathroom at school or play on the football team. Nobody understands how I feel. What can I do?

CHAPTER FIVE

Can You Hear Me Now? Standing for Change in a Sexist Society

People ask me sometimes...'When will there be enough women on the [Supreme] Court?' And my answer is 'When there are nine.'

—Ruth Bader Ginsburg, justice of the nine-member US Supreme Court

Why should you even worry about what happens in politics? After all, you can't even vote until you're eighteen (in some states you can vote in primary elections when you are seventeen.) But if coping with sexism and misogyny means that it needs to be recognized, understood, confronted, and exposed, then doing those things at the highest level could really make a difference.

The decisions politicians make greatly affect the lives of everyone in society. And the majority

Shown here is Supreme Court justice Ruth Bader Ginsburg.

of those politicians are men. They determine what kind of health care you can get; your rights in the workplace; funding for your education; when you, as a teen, can drive, drink, and vote; and to what extent you are protected in cases of sexual harassment or assault. To get fair representation on these issues and to right some of the gender inequalities that exist, there needs to be a greater representation of women in political office.

According to Equal Voice, a Canadian website advocating for women, "The United Nations says that a critical mass of at least 30 percent women is needed before legislatures produce public policy representing women's concerns and before political institutions begin to change the way they do business." In other words, the more women elected to political leadership roles, the more influence women will have on mitigating some of the effects of sexism and misogyny in our culture. That could affect you at school, at work, in public places, on public transportation, at colleges and universities, and on social media. But, as of 2017, both Canada and the United States have a long way to go before reaching that magic number. According to Rutgers: Eagleton Institute of Politics, in Canada, fewer than 25 percent of members of Parliaments are women. Across the nation, 25 percent of municipal seats are held by women, while only 16 percent of Canada's mayors are female.

Statistics in the United States are similar. In Congress, women make up 21 percent of the Senate and 19.1 percent of the House of Representatives. They comprise 24.8 percent of state legislatures, 20 percent of mayors, and 23.7 percent of statewide executives (governors, lieutenant governors, and other statewide elected officials). Equal Voice states that "there is still

Shown here is Kamala Lopez, director of *Equal Means Equal*, a film about why women seek passage of the Equal Rights Amendment in the United States.

stereotyping of women's role and abilities; media imbalances in the treatment of women politicians; and a rampant sexist perception of women's conduct and behavior."

In the United States, equal rights for women under the law is still not a reality (as of 2017) because the Equal Rights Amendment to the Constitution has never been ratified. According to Kamala Lopez, founder of the ERA Education Project, "Many young women today believe their rights are already protected. In fact, 75 percent to 90 percent of American women believe that the ERA already passed."

In reality, the ERA, written in 1923, and passed by Congress in 1972 but not ratified, still needs to be passed again by Congress and ratified by a majority of the states. Without it, discrimination against women is not specifically prohibited, leaving women vulnerable to judicial interpretation of their protections under the law.

More than 130 countries have laws protecting women from discrimination and Canada is one of them. The Canadian Charter of Rights and Freedoms specifically covers protection against gender discrimination. Its goal is to treat everyone equally, regardless of race, national or ethnic origin, color, religion, sex, age, mental or physical disability, sexual orientation, residency, marital status, or citizenship.

Many of the inequities, especially those in the workplace and sexual assault cases, could possibly be eliminated or reduced with the strength and support of an equal rights amendment in the United States. To find out how you can get involved, check out the educational program for students on Lopez's website: http://eraeducationproject.com.

Who, Me?

Most teens don't believe they can do anything to effect change, especially on a political level, until they are older. That's not necessarily true. If you do want to make a difference, there are some methods you might consider exploring now, such as joining organizations or getting politically active.

Political activism might sound like something for adults, but many teens are out there trying to make a difference. For example, in 2012, through a campaign on Change.org, teen girls pressured the media to include women as moderators at US presidential debates. It worked! Female political correspondents led two out of the four debates. And it continued; women also moderated during the 2016 debates.

According to an article on ShareAmerica, teens are getting involved politically all over the United States because they understand that they will soon be the ones taking on the roles of leadership of the country. In the same article, a high school boy tells kids his age why they should get involved now. "Do some homework. Pick a side. Discover your voice. There are lots of changes to be made to our government, so don't miss your chance to participate."

Beth Prescott, a teen who decided to get involved in politics, says there are no secrets or age barriers to being involved in politics. "There is just hard-work, determination and guts. The only barriers are the ones you convince yourself are there, even though they are not. The only thing stopping yourself from getting involved, is you."

Where Are All the Women (Statues)?

Women make up 50 percent of the US population, yet most streets, landmarks, and monuments are named after men. So some organizations formed to help balance out this inequity and increase the statues, streets, and landmarks named after women.

An initiative launched in 2017 called Put Her On the Map aims to get more statues, streets, and landmarks named after women. Their hope is that their efforts will result in reminding society of the many accomplishments of women.

(continued on the next page)

(continued from the previous page)

Pam Elam is the president of the Elizabeth Cady Stanton and Susan B. Anthony Statue Fund, an organization raising money to place statues of the suffragettes in New York City's Central Park. According to an article from New York Life, Elam said, "The real women who helped build this city, state and nation were nowhere to be found—until now. The Stanton and Anthony Woman Suffrage Movement Monument will ensure that many of the 42 million people who visit Central Park each year will become more aware of a history that fully and fairly includes the vast and varied roles women have played in it. Our statue project will honor all the women who fought for the vote."

In Canada, there is also a push for more public commemoration of women. In an article for Global News, spokesperson for the Halifax Women's History Society Janet Guildford said, "I guess I see it in part through my young granddaughter's eyes. As you walk through the city, only men are honoured and commemorated. Therefore, she must be less important than those men and I don't want her to grow up feeling like women don't make as big a contribution as men to any society. They certainly do and it's important to recognize that in a visual way."

Here are some ways you can get involved:

- Consider joining organizations like YouthVote.ca in Canada or FreeChild.org in the United States.
- Connect with a local politician during an election campaign or through the politician's website. Tell the politician what issues you care about.
- Volunteer to help a candidate during an election campaign; go to events and listen to what politicians have to say.

Want to make some changes? Peaceful protests and marches are just one way to make your voice heard about important political issues.

- Write articles for teen magazines that want to know what teens think about politics.
- Take part in boycotts and protests, with your parents' permission.
- Look into political science as a college major and consider running for office after you graduate.

Stand by Me

Besides becoming politically active and participating in various organizations, you can be an advocate for other students by calling out sexism at school, public places, or at work. Confronting and exposing sexism and misogyny is not easy, but it is one way of dealing with it; it can also be very empowering.

But speaking out or taking action when you see someone being victimized is risky and scary.

You don't always have to help at the time, especially if it's physically endangering for you to do so. But you can talk to the person attacked later and offer to listen or go with her as a witness to report the incident.

If you do want to do something more, there's a way to learn how. This strategy is called bystander intervention.

Jackson Katz heads up an organization called Mentors in Violence Prevention, or MVP. It's a bystander intervention program that "aims to train bystanders to feel enough compassion for female victims to act, whether by intervening to discourage attacks, offering aid, or calling authorities." The program has three goals:

"1) To help students and others develop a range of options for intervention in specific situations and scenarios;

2) To foster a peer culture ethos that motivates everyone to get involved in challenging and interrupting all forms of abuse, and helping to create a climate in which abusive attitudes, beliefs and behaviors are seen as unacceptable, uncool and unwelcome;

3) To help people of all ages and backgrounds develop the skills to become leaders and mentors to others on the issues of sexual assault and relationship abuse prevention."

According to Katz, "The goal is to use peer pressure to transform men and boys who participate in gender-based violence and humiliation into the outliers and those who speak up into the norm, instead of the other way around."

Katz says that "many people mistakenly believe that they have only two options in instances of actual or potential violence: intervene physically and possibly expose themselves to personal harm, or do nothing. As a result, they often choose to do nothing."

But those are not the only possible choices. The MVP model offers other options, most of which, according to Katz, "carry no risk of personal injury. With more options to choose from, people are more likely to respond and not be passive and silent—and hence complicit—in violence or abuse by others."

The MVP program might be one that would empower and help kids at your school. Check it out at www.mvpstrat.com.

Don't try to cope alone. If you or someone you know is a victim of sexism and misogyny, reach out to friends, family, an organization, or a professional.

Sexism and misogyny, by whatever names you choose to call them, still exist in the world today. Their victims may include all of us, but girls, women, and transgender teens are their biggest targets. Ignoring them perpetuates the problem and does nothing to mitigate the loss of self-worth and feelings of inadequacy and helplessness that are their by-products. Coping with them involves many different strategies. But whether you are dealing with them at home, at school, online, at work, in public spaces, in your personal relationships, or in all these places, the loudest message is this: *don't try to cope alone.* There are trustworthy, caring teens, adults, and organizations that are there to help you and are working to change the bigger picture. Find them. Join them. Get help. Get better. Then go make a difference.

Glossary

advocate To support or speak up for someone or something.

agency Taking action to control your life.

bystander intervention A program to teach and empower bystanders to help others who are victims of a sexist act.

chick flick A movie considered to be one that only girls would like.

double standard A rule or expectation that should apply to both genders but is only being accorded to one.

empower To make a person feel as though he or she has control.

feminist Anyone—man or woman—who stands up for gender equality.

gender bias Discrimination against a person based on whether they are male or female.

gender profiling Thinking of someone only in terms of preconceived ideas based on gender stereotypes.

manosphere A network of websites considered just for men.

mansplain To explain something to a woman in a condescending manner.

misogyny Hatred of or discrimination against women.

mitigate To reduce the effect of something.

objectification Considering a person as only an object, exclusive of anything else.

parity Equality, especially in reference to pay or status.

postfeminism Time following an era of feminism, in which its goals have been met.

sexism Discrimination based on whether a person is a man or a woman.

sexualization Looking at someone purely from a sexual viewpoint.

sissy A term sometimes used to mean a person is acting scared or "like a girl."

sissy bar A bar on the back of a motorcycle to keep the passenger from falling off.

tacit Suggested or implied without being said out loud.

transgender Having to do with someone whose internal understanding of who they are is a different gender from the one they were assigned at birth.

troll Someone who harasses others on social media to try to get a response.

vanilla Boring or not interesting.

For More Information

Canadian Women's Foundation
National office
133 Richmond St. W. Suite 504
Toronto, ON M5H 2L3
Canada
(416) 365-1444
Email: info@canadianwomen.org
Website: http://www.canadianwomen.org

The Canadian Women's Foundation is the country's only foundation devoted to providing better lives for women and girls of any income, race, religion, culture, physical ability, level of education, sexual orientation, or age. They strive to put an end to violence, make poverty a thing of the past, and empower all females.

Dove Self-Esteem Project
c/o Unilever US
700 Sylvan Ave
Englewood Cliffs, NJ 07632
(201) 894-4000
Website: http://www.selfesteem.dove.us
Facebook: @doveUS
Twitter: @dove

Instagram: @dove

The Dove Self-Esteem Project conducts workshops to foster in girls a positive relationship with their appearance and bodies, to raise self-esteem, and to help girls realize their full potential. Since the program began, they've taught seventeen million young people how to deal effectively with self-esteem issues.

4 Every Girl

707 Wilshire Boulevard

Suite 2075

Los Angeles, CA 90017

(213) 403-1325.

Website: http://www.4EveryGirl.com

Facebook: @4everygirl

Twitter: @4everygirl

4 Every Girl strives to change how media portrays girls and women. It's a campaign to encourage media industry leaders to present healthy, respectful representations of girls and women. They believe that beauty should be a source of confidence, not one of anxiety. One section offers a list of ways that girls can help with the campaign.

FreeChild Project

PO Box 6185

Olympia WA 98507-6185

(360) 489-9680

Email: info@freechild.org

Website: http://www.freechild.org

Facebook: @freechildproject

Twitter: @freechildprojec

Pinterest: @the-freechild-project

The Freechild Project is all about changing the world. Programs that address and work for change in the area of gender equality for boys and girls, both cisgender and transgender, is just one of the many issues this organization addresses.

Girls Action Foundation

24 Mont Royal West, Suite 601

Montreal, Quebec H2T 2S2

Canada

(888) 948-1112

Website: http://www.girlsactionfoundation.ca/en

Twitter: @_GirlsAction

Instagram: @girlsactionfoundation

Girls Action Foundation is a Canadian-based

nonprofit organization that develops programs that address the needs and issues facing girls through providing mentors, networks, and relevant resources.

Girls, Inc.

120 Wall Street

New York, NY 10005-3902

(212) 509-2000

Website: http://www.girlsinc.org

Facebook: @GirlsInc

Twitter: @girls_inc

Instagram: @girlsinc

YouTube: GirlsIncorporated

Girls Incorporated serves more than 140,000 girls ages six to eighteen in 350 cities across the United States and Canada. It educates and informs the media about girl-centric issues, as well as teaching girls how to become advocates themselves for positive change.

Girls for Gender Equity (GGE)

30 3rd Avenue, Suite 103

Brooklyn, NY 11217

(718) 857-1393 or (718) 857-1568

Website: http://www.ggenyc.org

Facebook: @girlsforgenderequity

Twitter: @GGENYC

YouTube: ggenyc

Girls for Gender Equity is an intergenerational organization dedicated to helping girls reach their potential. To that end, they have organized campaigns that address not only safety, but also equality on all levels, including social media and political and social arenas, such as school, public spaces, and work environments.

SPARK Movement

Colby College

4422 Mayflower Hill

Waterville, ME 04901

Email: dana@SPARKmovement.org or lyn@ SPARKmovement.org

Website: http://www.sparksummit.com

Facebook: @sparkmvmnt

Twitter: @sparkmvmnt

SPARK Movement works for gender justice and ending violence against women and girls, as well as empowerment of girls and women. Their girl-focused training teaches how to form coalitions and partnerships to make a difference in society and focuses on the individual lives of girls and women.

Websites

Because of the changing nature of internet links, Rosen Publishing has developed an online list of websites related to the subject of this book. This site is updated regularly. Please use this link to access this list:

http://www.rosenlinks.com/COP/Sexism

For Further Reading

Arrowsmith, Anna. *Rethinking Misogyny: Men's Perceptions of Female Power in Dating Relationships.* Farnham, UK: Ashgate, 2016.

Bancroft, Lundy. *Daily Wisdom for Why Does He Do That? Encouragement for Women Involved with Angry and Controlling Men.* New York, NY: Berkley, 2015.

Bates, Laura. *Everyday Sexism.* New York, NY: Thomas Dunne, St. Martin's Griffin, 2016.

Bray, Abigail. *Misogyny Re-loaded.* Chicago, IL: Spinifex, 2014.

David, Miriam E. *Reclaiming Feminism: Challenging Everyday Misogyny.* Bristol, UK: Policy, 2016.

Henneberg, Susan. *Gender Politics.* New York, NY: Greenhaven, 2017.

Jeffreys, Sheila. *Beauty and Misogyny Harmful Cultural Practices in the West.* Hove, East Sussex, UK: Routledge, Taylor & Francis Group, 2015.

Mableton, Barry, and Elizabeth Gettelman. *Basketball: Girls Rocking It.* New York, NY: Rosen Publishing, 2016.

Mantilla, Karla. *Gendertrolling: How Misogyny Went Viral.* Santa Barbara, CA: Praeger, 2015.

Mayock, Ellen C. *Gender Shrapnel in the Academic Workplace.* New York, NY: Palgrave Macmillan, 2016.

Petrikowski, Nicki Peter. *Gender Identity*. New York, NY: Rosen Publishing, 2014.

Ross, Michael Elsohn. *She Takes a Stand: 16 Fearless Activists Who Have Changed the World*. Chicago, IL: Chicago Review, 2015.

Valenti, Jessica. *Full Frontal Feminism: A Young Women's Guide to Why Feminism Matters*. Berkeley, CA: Seal, 2014.

Bibliography

Bates, Laura. *Everyday Sexism*. New York, NY: St. Martin's Press, 2016.

Bell, Taylor. "These High School Boys Hiked up Their Skirts to Protest Their School's Sexist Dress Code." The World Around Us, February 6, 2016. http://www.theworld-aroundus.com /others/world/these-high-school-boys-hiked -up-their-skirts-to-protest-their-schools -sexist-dress-code.

GirlTalkHQ. "Teen Girls: The Next Generation Tackling Gender Inequality Globally." Girls on a Mission blog, October 2, 2016. http://girltalkhq .com/teen-girls-the-next-generation-tackling -gender-inequality-globally.

Gregoire, Carolyn. "Julia Bluhm, 14, Leads Successful Petition For Seventeen Magazine To Portray Girls Truthfully." Huffington Post, July 5, 2012. http://www.huffingtonpost .com/2012/07/05/julia-bluhm-seventeen -mag_n_1650938.html.

Halvorson, Heidi Grant. "3 Reasons Why It Pays to Not Let Sexist Comments Slide." Forbes, October 3, 2011. https://www.forbes.com.

Leaper, Campbell, and Diana M. Arias. "College Women's Feminist Identity: A Multidimensional Analysis with Implications for Coping with Sexism." Sex Roles, April 2011. https://www .ncbi.nlm.nih.gov/pmc/articles/PMC3062025.

Meyer, Elizabeth J. *Gender, Bullying and Harassment: Strategies to End Sexism and Homophobia in Schools.* New York, NY: Teachers College Press, 2009.

MVP, Mentors in Violence Prevention. "Bystander Approach." Retrieved March 30, 2017. http://www.mvpnational.org/program-overview/bystander-approach.

Perle, Elizabeth. "Teen Feminism: 'The Day I Proved To My Class That Sexism Still Exists.'" Huffington Post, February 6, 2012. http://www.huffingtonpost.com/2012/02/06/the-8th-grade-feminist_n_1258670.html.

Pomerantz, Shauna, Rebecca Raby, and Anita Harris. *Smart Girls: Success, School, and the Myth of Post-Feminism.* Oakland, CA: University of California Press, 2017.

Rampton, John. "10 Tips to Dealing With Trolls." Forbes, April 9, 2015. https://www.forbes.com.

Rutgers: Eagleton Institute of Politics. "Current Numbers." Center for American Women and Politics (CAWP). Retrieved March 30, 2017. http://www.cawp.rutgers.edu/current-numbers.

Sales, Nancy Jo. *American Girls: Social Media and the Secret Lives of Teenagers.* New York, NY: Vintage, 2017.

ShareAmerica. "In Politics, Teens Discover Their Voices." ShareAmerica, October 20, 2016.

https://share.america.gov/in-politics-teens
-discover-their-voices.

Tannenbaum, Melanie. "The Problem When
Sexism Just Sounds So Darn Friendly..."
Scientific American Blog Network, August
6, 2013. https://blogs.scientificamerican.com
/psysociety/benevolent-sexism.

Thompson, Lisa. "Sexism and Social Media: What
It's Like to be a Teenager Today." Self Love Beauty,
August 21, 2016. http://www.selflovebeauty
.com/2016/04/sexism-and-social-media.

Vagianos, Alanna. "Adorable Girls Sum Up Why We
Need More Landmarks Named After Women."
Huffington Post, February 14, 2017. http://www
.huffingtonpost.com/entry/adorable-girls-sum
-up-why-we-need-more-landmarks-named
-after-women_us_58a31e6ce4b0ab2d2b19223c.

Watson, Stephanie. "Dealing With Mean Girls
in High School and Middle School." WebMD,
November 22, 2010. http://teens.webmd.com
/girls/features/dealing-with-mean-girls#1.

Yi, Jacqueline. "The Role of Benevolent Sexism
in Gender Inequality." Applied Psychology
OPUS—NYU Steinhardt. Retrieved March 30,
2017. http://steinhardt.nyu.edu/appsych/opus
/issues/2015/spring/yi.

Index

A

advocate, 64, 92
agency, 65, 75
American Psychological
    Association, 21
appearance, 19, 50, 69
Ardsley, Hannah S., 36
Association of American
    University Women
    (AAUW), 63, 64

B

Ban Bossy, 55
Barbie dolls, 18,19
Barlow, Gary, 74
Bates, Laura, 21, 24, 57, 60
Beyoncé, 13, 54, 55
Boston Review, 16
Burleigh, Nina, 75
Buzzfeed, 50
bystander intervention, 92

C

chick flick, 6
Childnet, 74
cisgender people, 14, 24, 57
Cleveland, Lydia, 40
college campuses, 47, 60–61
Cook, Hera, 30–31

D

Daley, Tom, 72
dating, 18, 28, 41–43,
Davis, Geena, 13

discrimination, 6, 9, 11, 15,
    16, 19, 34, 36, 50, 56, 57,
    63, 64, 87
Disney, 19
double standard, 33, 34
Dove Self-Esteem Project, 25
dress code, 4, 33, 36, 37, 39, 40
Drimonis, Toula, 34

E

Equal Rights Amendment,
    ERA, 87–88
empowerment, 8, 26, 63, 64,
    74, 92, 94
Eudey, Betsy, 59
Everyday Sexism, 24

F

Facebook, 67, 68, 75, 77
family, 28–32
feminist, 11, 13
Fiske, Susan, 16, 48

G

Gardner, Will, 74
Garner, Jennifer, 69
gender bias, 51, 64
*Gender, Bullying and
    Harassment: Strategies
    to End Sexism and
    Homophobia in
    Schools*, 32
gender profiling, 41
Girls & Sex: Navigating

*the Complicated New
Landscape*, 68
Girls Scouts Research
Institute, 21
Glick, Peter, 15–16, 48

H

*He's a Stud, She's a Slut and 49
Other Double Standards
Every Woman Should
Know*, 59

I

Instagram, 67

J

jock, 34

K

Kaiser, Cheryl R., 63
Katz, Jackson, 75, 92–94
Kirkpatrick, Jessica, 51, 53

L

Laville, Sandra, 77
LeanIn.org, 53
Lopez, Kamala, 87, 88

M

Manne, Kate, 16
manosphere, 67
mansplain, 61
Marquette University, 28

McKinley & Co., 53
Media Education
Foundation, 24
Mentors in Violence
Prevention (MVP), 75,
92, 94
Meyer, Elizabeth J., 33
Miller, Carol T., 63
misogyny, 6, 7, 15, 16, 18, 24,
28, 60, 65, 67, 68, 72, 75,
77, 83, 85, 92, 95
Myspace, 77

N

National Organization for
Women (NOW), 33
Nixon, Charisse, 24, 77, 80

O

objectification, 18, 19, 24, 44,
65, 68
Orenstein, Peggy, 68

P

parity, 53
patriarchy, 16
Phillips, Jess, 70
Pomerantz, Shauna, 33, 37,
51, 53
postfeminism, 4
prejudice, 6, 9, 15
Prescott, Beth, 89
public spaces, 47, 56, 57, 59, 95

R

Raby, Rebecca, 33, 51, 53
Reclaim the Internet, 70
Reddit, 67
relationships, 41, 68, 93, 95

S

Sales, Nancy Jo, 65, 68
Samsa, Ashley Lauren, 34
school, 6, 13, 15, 16, 19, 21,
    28, 32, 33, 34, 36, 37, 39,
    40, 41, 45, 47, 51, 57, 60,
    77, 85, 88, 92, 94, 95
sexism, 4, 6, 7, 9, 11, 13, 15,
    28, 32, 34, 36, 41, 45, 51,
    54, 56, 57, 59, 60, 61, 63,
    64, 65, 67, 68, 77, 83, 85,
    92, 95
sexual harassment, 6, 18, 47,
    70, 84
sexualization, 19, 68
sissy bar, 6
Smart Girls, 33, 51
Snapchat, 67
social media, 6, 16, 18, 19,
    65, 67, 68, 70, 72, 77,
    78, 80, 85
SPARK, 25, 26
*Statistical Overview of Women
    in the Workforce*, 53
Steffens, Melanie C., 47
Stein, Joel, 72
STEM, 61, 64
Stop Street Harassment
    (SSH), 57, 59, 60

T

Tatum, Erin, 41
Teen Ink, 36
Title IX, 36
transgender people, 4, 6, 7,
    11, 14, 17, 18, 24, 33, 36,
    37, 57, 74, 95
troll, 72, 74, 75
Twitter, 44, 67, 68, 72, 75, 77

U

University of Melbourne, 54
USA Today Network, 18

V

Valenti, Jessica, 59
vanilla, 68
Viladot, Maria Angels, 47

W

Watson, Emma, 13
workplace, 6, 16, 45, 47, 48,
    50, 51, 56, 64, 67, 75, 77,
    84, 85, 87, 88, 92, 95

Y

Yale University, 48
YCteen, 16
Yi, Jacqueline, 48

About the Author

Gloria G. Adams is a former librarian who is a writer, women's rights advocate, and partner in a children's book manuscript critique and editing business, Two-4-One Kid Critiques. She has been published in magazines and anthologies and has worked as a compiling editor for Greenhaven Press. Her published children's works include *Ah-Choo!*, with co-author Lana Wayne Koehler, and *My Underpants Are Made from Plants*, with Vera J. Hurst. Adams is also a member of the Society of Children's Book Writers and Illustrators.

Photo Credits